Original title:

Inlaid Trinkets Among the Mermaid Pane

Author: Paula Raudsepp

ISBN HARDBACK: 978-1-80559-368-3

ISBN PAPERBACK: 978-1-80559-867-1

Jewels of the Deep

In the twilight, treasures gleam,
Colors dance, a sailor's dream.
Coral crowns and shells so rare,
Beneath the waves, beyond compare.

Fins shimmer past, a fleeting sight,
Underneath the moon's soft light.
Hidden gems in ocean's swell,
Each tide tells a tale to tell.

Anemones sway with grace,
In this vast and serene place.
Whispers echo through the blue,
Secrets held by waters true.

The depths hold stories yet untold,
In currents warm and currents cold.
Life blooms in a silent sweep,
In this realm, the jewels keep.

Dangers lurk where shadows creep,
Yet beauty thrives in waters deep.
In the heart of the ocean's throng,
The jewels of the deep belong.

Echoes of the Sea Glass

Fragments glisten on the shore,
Stories whispered, tales of yore.
Colors swirled in sunlit hue,
Echoes of the waves they knew.

Once shattered dreams in brine did sink,
Now polished smooth, they softly wink.
The past and present intertwine,
In shards of glass, a truth divine.

Each piece speaks of journeys long,
Of tides that ebb and flow so strong.
Wind and water made their claim,
Yet still they shine, despite the pain.

Nature's art in hues so bright,
Capturing the heart's delight.
In every shard, a moment cast,
Echoes of the sea, steadfast.

From ocean's depths to sandy curls,
The world unfolds in gentle swirls.
In the art of time and space,
The sea reveals its hidden grace.

Whispers Beneath the Waves

Beneath the surface, silence hums,
Secrets flow as the ocean drums.
Echoes linger in the deep,
In gentle tones, the waters weep.

Creatures dance in ghostly flight,
A ballet rich in mystic light.
Coral gardens bloom and fade,
In this realm, the magic's made.

Softly gliding through the night,
Shadows flicker, a wondrous sight.
In briny depths, life holds its breath,
Whispers sing of love and death.

Tangled in the kelp's embrace,
Memories drift, a tranquil space.
Listening close to the ocean's sigh,
Secrets drift as currents fly.

In twilight hours, the heart connects,
With unseen loves and deep respects.
In the hush below the foam,
The whispers always find a home.

Tides of Celestial Wonders

The moon commands the rolling tide,
Celestial dance, the stars abide.
Waves that shimmer with silver glow,
In the night, a gentle flow.

Each pulse tells of cosmic dreams,
Infinite paths in glistening beams.
The universe in ocean's frame,
Connected hearts that feel the same.

As stars are mirrored in the sea,
Each wave a song, a symphony.
In the vastness, we are small,
Yet in this magic, we stand tall.

Whispers carry on the breeze,
Secrets shared with timeless ease.
The tides reveal their hidden lore,
Of wonders resting on the shore.

In the ebb and flow of fate,
We find our place, we celebrate.
In every drop, a world so grand,
The tides of wonders, hand in hand.

Echoes of Luminous Beneath

Whispers dance on the water's skin,
Reflections float where shadows begin.
Footsteps trace the twilight shore,
As echoes linger, forevermore.

Stars descend in a soft embrace,
Painting night with a gentle grace.
Glow of secrets, bright yet shy,
Infinite wishes, like stars, fly high.

Waves sing songs of the lost and found,
In moonlit dreams, our hearts are bound.
Quiet moments, a shared glance,
Life's fleeting beauty, in a trance.

Tides carry tales from far away,
Cascading stories that long to stay.
In silence deep, we hear them call,
Nature's secrets wrapped in thrall.

Above the depths, the light will weave,
A tapestry that we believe.
In echoes soft, our spirits blend,
And with each wave, the tales ascend.

Adornments from a Dreamy Veil

Petals fall like whispers in the night,
Softly landing in the silver light.
Jewels scatter on the waking ground,
Each a promise, a love profound.

Fanciful visions in the twilight glow,
Woven together in the currents low.
Glimmers sparkle in the sleepy air,
Crafting dreams that linger, rare.

Laces of mist entangle the trees,
Catching secrets left by the breeze.
Fragrant echoes of the day gone by,
Lifting spirits as they float and fly.

In the heart of twilight, a whisper grows,
As time unfolds, its beauty shows.
Draped in wonder, we find our place,
Wrapped in each other's warm embrace.

Through tapestry threads of twilight we roam,
Finding joy in a world like home.
Each adornment, a story shared,
In the dreamy veil, our hearts bared.

Lunar Tears on the Silken Surface

Luna weeps in the still of night,
Her tears shimmer with silver light.
Resting softly on velvet waves,
Each drop tender, each moment saves.

Waves caress the twinkling shore,
As shadows dance, they ask for more.
Brushing gently with the moon's warm glow,
A silent story only they know.

Reflecting dreams in pools of calm,
The ocean's whispers, a soothing balm.
Ripples carry tales of the vast,
As time flows on, forever cast.

Night's embrace cradles the weary,
In lunar light, the soul feels cheery.
Graceful movements, a serene affair,
In the night's beauty, we find our prayer.

Silken surface, cloaked in peace,
Each lunar tear grants sweet release.
In liquid diamonds, our hopes align,
Under the watchful gaze divine.

Fantasies of Depth and Light

In the cavern where shadows play,
Light and darkness weave their ballet.
Dreams unfurl in the silent deep,
Mystical wonders awaken from sleep.

Layers of color swell and breathe,
In every wave, a world we leave.
Fantasies drift on currents strong,
Each moment captured in a song.

Roots entwined in the earth's embrace,
Whispering secrets in a sacred space.
Stories told in the flickering spark,
Illuminating paths through the dark.

Rippling echoes in the ocean's sprawl,
Painting tales along the walls.
In every layer, a truth unfolds,
A dance of light in the dark it holds.

Timeless treasures beneath our feet,
In depths profound, we feel complete.
Fantasies flourish, wild and free,
Where depth meets light, we long to be.

Echoing Secrets of the Abyss

Whispers linger in the dark,
Silent tales from depths below,
Fragments of a time long past,
Secrets that the shadows know.

Waves will carry words of woe,
Moons will rise to hear them sigh,
Journeys lost to darkened tides,
In the depths where echoes lie.

Fading songs of ancient ships,
Rust and relics wrapped in night,
Beneath the weight of endless blue,
A chorus lost from human sight.

Ghostly figures dance in dreams,
Guiding souls through watery graves,
Their stories stitch the ocean's seams,
As time flows deep like rolling waves.

In every rise and fall of tide,
A memory, a haunting call,
Beneath the foam, the echoes hide,
In the abyss, they sing for all.

Beneath the Silvery Sway

Softly glimmering, the sea,
Draws us close to its embrace,
Dancing lightly, waves at play,
Glistening under moon's soft grace.

The whispers of the ocean's breath,
Carry tales of lovers lost,
Each swell a gentle lullaby,
A calling that we can't exhaust.

Over ripples, shadows glide,
While stars reflect on liquid skies,
Beneath the calm, all secrets hide,
In silence, where the heart complies.

Veils of silver, spun from dreams,
In the quiet, stories dwell,
Unraveled threads of whispered schemes,
As varied as the ocean's shell.

So let the tide and moon conspire,
To weave their magic 'neath the sway,
In every wave, a fleeting fire,
That lights the night, as dreams delay.

Constellations in Marine Whirls

Beneath the waves, stars align,
Twinkling fish in cosmic dance,
Swirling currents, paths divine,
In the depths, we find our trance.

Octopus, with jeweled skin,
Writes stories through the silken sea,
While drifting sands, soft and thin,
Map the constellations, free.

Coral castles hold their breath,
Guardians of the ocean's lore,
Each vibrant hue, a tale of death,
Of life reborn from ocean floor.

In every tide's relentless sweep,
A promise hidden in the swell,
With every secret, oceans keep,
A universe prepared to tell.

Stars now shift to guide the way,
Through marine whirls, we wander on,
In endless depths, the night will stay,
As constellations lead to dawn.

The Lure of Forgotten Shells

In tangled seaweed, shells conceal,
Whispers of the tides long gone,
Silent stories, time will heal,
Each finds a lover in the dawn.

On sandy shores where dreams collide,
Ocean's bounty waits for hands,
In the hunt, we seek and glide,
Collecting treasures from the sands.

Cracked and worn, their beauty lies,
Imprints of a life they've led,
Each one a truth, beneath the skies,
A memory of ocean's bed.

With every spiral, every hue,
A traveler's path is outlined,
Beneath the sun, the shells renew,
Whispering tales of those entwined.

So let us wander, hearts unfurled,
In the rhythm of the tide's swell,
For every shell holds a lost world,
A song of love, the ocean's spell.

Gems Beneath the Ocean's Floor

Beneath the waves, the treasures lie,
Glints of light in shadows shy.
Whispers of the deep sea's dance,
Echo secrets in a trance.

Emeralds rest in sandy beds,
Sapphires glow where silence spreads.
With each tide that pulls and sways,
The ocean tells its layered ways.

Drifting softly, time does weave,
A tapestry of dreams we leave.
In every shell, a story's spun,
Of distant shores and of the sun.

Where playful dolphins weave their art,
Beneath the surface, nature's heart.
Finding peace in watery roam,
The ocean's gems feel like home.

Together we share this watery song,
With every tide, we all belong.
Treasures found, let memories soar,
Beneath the waves, forevermore.

Enchanted Shells and Whispered Tides

Shells aglow in morning light,
Whispered secrets, pure delight.
Each curve holds a tale untold,
Of restless waves and waters bold.

Emerald greens and coral reds,
Nature's canvas, beauty spreads.
Every shell, a kissed farewell,
Of wanderers who dared to dwell.

Tides that dance on silver sands,
Calling forth from distant lands.
Echoes of the past reside,
In every shell, the ocean's pride.

Moonlit nights and starry skies,
Where the ocean softly sighs.
Each crest a promise, each ebb a kiss,
In listening waves, we find our bliss.

Bound by dreams, we sail along,
In the chorus of the sea's song.
With enchanted shells in our hands,
We become part of the strands.

Secrets of the Coral Cavern

In coral caverns, colors blend,
Life entwined, where currents bend.
Hidden depths hold quiet grace,
A sanctuary, a sacred place.

Fish weave tales through twisted lanes,
In the hush of ocean veins.
Whispers float, the water speaks,
Of ancient wisdom, true mystique.

Every crevice hides a clue,
Of nature's art in every hue.
Fragile fingers trace the walls,
Hear the siren's call that enthralls.

Beneath the surface, worlds collide,
With playful echoes as our guide.
Lessons learned in silence deep,
In coral caverns, memories sleep.

Together here, we dive and find,
The secrets that the sea has lined.
In the quiet, we are free,
To embrace ocean's mystery.

Starlight Reflections in Sea Glass

Fragments caught in ocean's hand,
Polished treasures from the sand.
Whispers glow in twilight's gleam,
A starlit dance, a waking dream.

Each piece tells a story bold,
Of journeys long, of magic old.
Caught in waves, then cast aside,
Now shining bright with ocean's pride.

Reflections dance beneath the moon,
A melody, a soothing tune.
Softly humming, they respond,
To gentle tides of an endless bond.

In twilight's grasp, we find delight,
As sea glass sparkles in the night.
Memories blend with nature's art,
Each shard a map to the heart.

Together we wander, hand in hand,
Across this shimmering, glassy land.
With starlight guiding the way we pass,
In dreams awakened by sea glass.

Trophies from a Siren's Lament

Once I heard her haunting song,
Echoes lingered all night long.
Gems and shells, treasures rare,
Whispered secrets, caught in her snare.

Lost voices drift on the breeze,
Heartfelt tales, carried with ease.
Each note weaves a story told,
Of loves found and dreams bold.

From dark waves where shadows play,
Siren's tears wash dreams away.
Trophies gleam in moonlit glow,
Fleeting moments, swift to go.

In twilight's grip, secrets arise,
Across the vast, glittering skies.
A haunting beauty lingers still,
Trophies of sorrow, dreams to fulfill.

With each whisper, time stands still,
Heartbeats echo, chasing the thrill.
These captured treasures hold the lore,
Of sirens lost, forevermore.

The Dance of Shadows in Ocean Depths

In the depths where silence dwells,
Water's secret, it gently tells.
Shadows glide in a graceful trance,
Mysteries deep, in a whispered dance.

Beneath blue, the world is strange,
Formless shapes in endless range.
A ballet of light, flickering bright,
Soft whispers float through the endless night.

Currents twirl, weaving their art,
Crafting dreams from ocean's heart.
Footfalls fade in the watery gloom,
As shadows bloom in aquatic room.

Ghostly figures sway and spin,
Life and death entwined within.
Echoed laughter of the lost,
Every movement counts the cost.

In tidal rhythms, secrets play,
The dance of shadows leads the way.
Lost and found, in depths we roam,
Where shadows gather, we are home.

Fragments of Myths in Seashell Residue

By the shore, the tales unwind,
Ancient stories, lost in time.
Seashell whispers fill the air,
Fragments of myths, treasures rare.

Each ripple holds a timeless fable,
Of mermaids fair and ships unstable.
In every curve, a story lies,
Reflecting dreams beneath the skies.

From ocean's womb, the echoes call,
A lullaby from the silent thrall.
Seashells, keepers of the deep,
Guarding scribed secrets that we keep.

Tides will change, but legends stay,
Woven in grains, they softly play.
By starlit shores, where we convene,
The seashells sing of what has been.

Fragments of myths in the sand,
Carved by nature's gentle hand.
Listen close, let your heart lead,
To the stories where dreams succeed.

Lost Relics of the Briny Deep

Where shipwrecks lie in slumber deep,
Whispers of the ocean keep.
Lost relics tell of battles past,
In coral gardens, shadows cast.

Rusting anchors hold the tales,
Of sailors brave, of squalls and gales.
Quicksilver currents carry loss,
In depths where fortune paid the cost.

Through murky depths, we seek the light,
Treasures hidden, lost from sight.
Each find reveals a forgotten name,
In the briny deep, we play the game.

Fragments of time and weathered wood,
Where dreams sailed and legends stood.
Buried secrets in ocean's clasp,
Await the touch of a curious grasp.

Through the waves, the past we trace,
Unearthed relics hold their place.
In the briny depths, stories sleep,
Forever ours, their secrets keep.

Adornments Lost to Time's Currents

Jewels of the past, they shimmer dim,
Forgotten treasures, on a whim.
Each delicate thread, a tale concealed,
In silence, their stories are revealed.

Waves lap softly on the shore,
Whispers of sailors, legends of yore.
Fragments of gold, in the sand they lie,
Adornments lost to the vast, blue sky.

The tide pulls back, revealing the land,
Dancing shadows that time has planned.
Echoes of laughter, so faint yet clear,
In the hearts of those who hold them dear.

Seashells sing with a muted tone,
History's brush has gently sewn.
Silent witnesses to joys and sighs,
Adornments lost where memory lies.

As the sun sets, colors ignite,
Fleeting moments in beautiful light.
Time flows onward, but dreams remain,
In the currents of love, joy, and pain.

Fables Cradled in Coral Dreams

Beneath the waves, the fables weave,
Coral cradles what we believe.
Stories of mermaids and long-lost ships,
Whispers of magic on ocean's lips.

In the twilight, soft shadows flow,
Secrets hidden where aquatic flowers grow.
Each creature a keeper, each wave a note,
In the symphony of seas, they softly wrote.

Glimmers of sunlight dance on the reef,
Tales interwoven, a shared belief.
The ancients speak through the tides' refrain,
Fables cradled in the gentle rain.

Crimson and blue, a vibrant embrace,
Life in the depths, a mystical space.
They anchor our dreams where light meets dark,
In the heart of the ocean, a flickering spark.

At night, the stars reflect in the deep,
Guardians of stories, secrets they keep.
In this realm of wonder, we'll forever sway,
Fables cradled, our hearts will stay.

The Enchantment of Hidden Shores

Whispers of land, where the sky meets sea,
Hidden shores call, enchanting me.
Footprints in sand lead to mysteries rare,
Magic woven in the cool, salty air.

Coves that cradle the secrets untold,
Glimmers of treasure more precious than gold.
Each breeze a story, each tide a song,
In the dance of the waves, we find where we belong.

The horizon blushes with colors aglow,
As the sun dips low, painting shadows below.
Shells like laughter, scattered with care,
Echo the secrets the sea wishes to share.

Dunes shift softly, in twilight's embrace,
Time stands still in this breathtaking space.
The world outside fades, and here we dwell,
Under the spell of the ocean's sweet sell.

Every moment a treasure, every glance a gift,
In the arms of the waves, our spirits uplift.
Lost in the charm of the shores we adore,
Together forever, forevermore.

Secrets Carried by Tidal Breezes

Tidal breezes dance, secrets they bring,
In their gentle sway, we hear them sing.
Lush whispers of past, in each soft flow,
Tales of the ocean, only we know.

As the waves play a serenade soft,
Stories unfold as the sailboats loft.
Drifting through time, the sea carries fate,
In the heart of the storm, we patiently wait.

Crashing surf mingles with dreams of the night,
Guiding lost souls into morning light.
Secrets entwined with the rise and fall,
Voices of nature's eternal call.

Each gust a reminder of things left unsaid,
In the currents they flow, where lovers have bled.
The salt on our lips, the breeze in our hair,
Holding each secret with delicate care.

So let us embrace what the tides impart,
The stories of waters, the depths of the heart.
With each ebb and flow, we rise and we roam,
Secrets of life, we carry them home.

Ocean's Fabled Adornments

Waves brush treasures from the deep,
Shells and jewels in silence keep.
Colors dance in twilight's glow,
Nature's gems in ebb and flow.

Whispers of the tides intone,
Secrets where the sea foam's blown.
Starfish, coral, tales unfold,
In this world of wonders bold.

Mirrors of the ocean's grace,
Time stands still in this warm embrace.
Beneath the shimmering surface lies,
A realm where magic never dies.

Veiled in mist, the cove will sing,
Of all the joys the sea can bring.
In shadows deep, the stories play,
Of sea-bound dreams that drift away.

Glistening treasures on the sand,
Touching hearts, like a gentle hand.
When daylight fades and stars appear,
The ocean's secrets whisper near.

Mysteries Laid Bare in Seaglass

Fragments of time, smoothed by the tide,
Stories hidden within them hide.
Colors mingling, lost and found,
In the silence, secrets abound.

Crushed by waves, yet still they gleam,
Echoes of an ancient dream.
A bottle's whisper, a sailor's sigh,
In every shard, a lullaby.

Underneath the moonlit sky,
These wonders beckon, catch the eye.
Ghosts of journeys come alive,
As each shard tells how it arrived.

Worn smooth by currents, touched by fate,
Each piece a story, intricate.
Together they form a tapestry,
Of resilience, hope, and mystery.

Lies the magic of the sea,
In seaglass treasures, wild and free.
Hold them close, let tales unfurl,
In every gleam, a hidden world.

Nautical Whispers of Forgotten Lore

Beneath the waves, where shadows dwell,
Ancient mariners weave their spell.
Echoes carry through the foam,
Sailing souls who roam the gloam.

Lost ships whisper through the night,
Guiding dreams with silver light.
Tales of storms and love once bright,
Now drift gently, out of sight.

Message in a bottle's plea,
Worn like an old, familiar key.
Ports of call, long left behind,
In the ocean's depths, we find.

Secrets lingering in the mist,
Memories that long exist.
In every ripple, in every wave,
The nautical whispers of the brave.

Hark! The call of deep, blue seas,
Draws us close, like a soft, sweet breeze.
In the heart of the ocean's core,
Are whispers rich with ancient lore.

The Glistening Respite of the Abyss

Where light and dark in silence meet,
Resting softly, the ocean's heartbeat.
Depths revealing what time forgot,
In the abyss, a tranquil spot.

Stars descend in liquid dreams,
As the world glimmers, shadowed beams.
A hidden realm, serene and vast,
Where whispers of the past are cast.

Echoes dance through the silent gloom,
Life abounds in the ocean's womb.
Creatures glide where few have seen,
In the stillness, a bond unseen.

An embrace of deep sapphire hues,
Cradling tales of timeless views.
Feeling small, yet part of this,
In the abyss, we find our bliss.

Respite in the depths, we yearn,
In ocean's cradle, tides will turn.
Glimmers beckon from the floor,
In the abyss, we seek and soar.

Treasures of the Sunken Realm

Beneath the waves, where shadows dwell,
Gold and jewels cast their spell.
Sunken ships, tales untold,
Whispers of fortunes, glimmers of gold.

Seashells cradling secrets deep,
Where lost dreams and wishes sleep.
Coral gardens, silent and grand,
Hold the treasures of a forgotten land.

Echoes of sailors' hearts entwined,
In watery graves, stories aligned.
Mermaids sing through ripples bright,
Guiding the brave through darkest night.

The compass spins, a map unclear,
Yet adventure calls, draws us near.
With daring souls, we take the dive,
For in the depths, true dreams come alive.

In the sunken realm, we seek and find,
A dance with legends, forever entwined.
Through darkened waters, we roam free,
Unraveling the past, just you and me.

Siren's Call to Forgotten Riches

A haunting song upon the breeze,
Lured by whispers among the trees.
Where the ocean meets the shore,
Siren's call beckons for more.

In swirling depths, the treasures lay,
Guarded by spirits, come what may.
Lost to time, yet within reach,
A promise found, no words to teach.

With every wave, the secrets flow,
Tales of heartache, longing, and woe.
Glint of silver, shimmer of gold,
Ancient stories waiting to be told.

Through storms and shadows we sail bold,
Chasing dreams, our fate foretold.
To seize the moment, embrace the thrill,
To honor the past, to bend our will.

The siren's call is rich and clear,
Drawing us closer, we persevere.
For in the depths, our fates are spun,
To claim the riches, to be the one.

Reflections in the Glassy Tide

The tide rolls in, a mirror unfolds,
Capturing stories, secrets untold.
Reflections dance on a shimmering bed,
Of dreams and wishes, long since dead.

Beneath the surface, shadows shift,
Souls of the ocean, tides they gift.
Lost sailors' faces, a fleeting glance,
Each ripple a memory, lost in a trance.

The moonlight glimmers, a silver thread,
Stitching the night where the brave have led.
In glassy depths, our hopes align,
As waters weave tales of fate divine.

Fishes dart, a bright ballet,
In the tides of time, they sway and play.
With ebb and flow, they sing their song,
In reflections of where we all belong.

So dive with me, into the shine,
Let's capture the moments, intertwine.
In the glassy tide, we find our way,
In water's embrace, we'll forever stay.

The Enchantment of Submerged Secrets

Silence falls where waters gleam,
Beneath the waves lies a hidden dream.
Secrets cradle in the ocean's heart,
Whispers of stories that never depart.

Ancient ruins call through the night,
Twisting paths in the fading light.
Every current carries a tale,
Of lost beginnings, a ghostly trail.

With lanterns held high, we dive beneath,
In search of treasures, untouched, unsheathed.
The melody of the deep enthralls,
As each submerged secret softly calls.

Bubbles rise in a gentle embrace,
In the stillness, we find our place.
The enchantment glows, a soft, sweet hum,
Inviting us closer, we're never numb.

With every breath, the depths surprise,
In the underwater realm, our spirits rise.
For in the silence, enchantments thrive,
In submerged secrets, we come alive.

Shells That Hold Celestial Stories

In the soft embrace of sandy shore,
Whispers of oceans call, forevermore.
Each shell cradles tales from the sea's heart,
Echoing secrets, where dreams intertwine and part.

Stars in their spirals, a cosmic dance,
Shimmering stories of fate and chance.
The moon's silver touch, on tides it descends,
Guides lost sailors till daylight lends.

Carved in the colors of twilight's sigh,
Shells hold the truths of the sea and sky.
A lullaby sung by the waves so deep,
Where memories linger and twilight dreams creep.

Crimson and azure, their beauty unspun,
Fragments of light where horizons run.
Gather these treasures, let them unfold,
Shells that embrace tales both new and old.

My heart finds solace on this tranquil shore,
Listening to stories—forever I explore.
In each tiny shell, a universe swells,
Holding celestial fables, as time gently dwells.

Trinkets from the Depths of Dream

Beneath the waves, where shadows play,
Trinkets lie waiting, hidden away.
Fragments of dreams in surf's gentle clasp,
Moments suspended, in time's tender grasp.

Seashells glazed with night's deep hue,
Bearing reflections of stars shining through.
With each gentle wave, they whisper and gleam,
A treasure trove born from the depths of dream.

Coral and stones, with stories untold,
Secrets of oceans in colors so bold.
Each trinket a memory, a wish set free,
Carried by currents, from sea to the sea.

The tide brings treasures, both strange and divine,
In pools of reflection, their stories entwine.
In the hush of the ocean, where silence lays,
Lie trinkets from dreams of forgotten days.

Collecting these wonders, my heart sings so bright,
Each piece tells a tale, a spark of delight.
From the depths of dream, they rise to my hand,
Trinkets of love from a magical land.

Glistening Flotsam on Celestial Waters

Waves lift the treasures, shining alight,
Glistening flotsam in the soft moonlight.
Drifting and dancing on the wild tide,
A ballet of wonders that never can hide.

Fragments of laughter and whispers of dreams,
Cradled by waters, where starlight redeems.
Nature's confetti, in twinkling displays,
Floating and swirling in infinite ways.

Glass and seaweed, a shimmering show,
Carried by currents, where soft breezes blow.
Each treasure reflects, in its radiant glow,
The secrets of oceans that ebb and flow.

In the quiet of dusk, the surface alive,
With a tapestry woven, where shadows thrive.
Glistening flotsam, a tapestry spun,
A dance of the ocean, where sea meets sun.

I gather these wonders, each glint and each fade,
The stories they tell in the twilight parade.
On celestial waters, my spirit takes flight,
Finding my place in the soft, starlit night.

Celestial Finds Beneath Aquatic Veils

Beneath the waves, where the world turns slow,
Celestial finds in currents that flow.
Aquatic veils of turquoise and green,
Hold ancient mysteries, unseen and serene.

Glimmers of gold in shadows entwined,
Echoes of silence, a sacred bind.
Findings of beauty in the ocean's cradle,
Awakening wonder like an ancient fable.

Sea glass and shells, remnants of grace,
Tales of the depths in each fragile space.
The dance of the light, with a shimmer divine,
Capturing moments where stars intertwine.

Wander the tides, let them guide your gaze,
To treasures submerged in a watery haze.
Each find a promise of dreams to explore,
In aquatic veils, so rich at the core.

With every discovery, my heart stirs anew,
The songs of the sea like whispers so true.
Celestial finds that the deep oceans yield,
Awakening spirits, a mystery revealed.

Nautical Dreams Entwined in Echoes

In whispered winds, they softly sway,
Beneath the stars, lost in the fray.
A vessel sails on memories' streams,
Caught in the web of nautical dreams.

Waves crash gently, secrets unfold,
Echoes of legends, tales of old.
With every tide, a promise sways,
In the ocean's heart, where silence plays.

Shadows dance on the moonlit swell,
A siren's song, a mystic spell.
The compass spins, in night's embrace,
Leading the soul to a sacred place.

Drifting softly, hope ignites,
In quiet depths, where love unites.
Through somber depths, the dreams aspire,
Like whispers caught in a smoky choir.

With every voyage, new shores call,
The heart flows free, yet fears to fall.
Eclipsed by fears, yet still they roam,
These nautical dreams forever home.

The Allure Beyond the Horizon's Reach

Chasing the dawn where the sea meets sky,
The call of adventure, a breathless sigh.
Golden rays paint the rippling blue,
Awakening wonders, familiar and new.

Wonders unseen, beyond the familiar,
Echoing dreams, emotions stir clearer.
Sailing towards what the heart yearns,
While every wave has a story that turns.

Current and breeze weave tales untold,
Mapping the heart with desires bold.
Glimmers of fate whisper through the air,
In the embrace of the ocean's care.

From distant shores, tales of the brave,
In the depths where legends still wave.
Each longing glance at the vast unknown,
Unravel the feelings we've always known.

As twilight descends, the night unfolds,
Secrets of stars, and stories retold.
With passion igniting, hearts will sear,
In the allure of dreams, we hold so dear.

Festooned by Ocean's Embrace

A tapestry woven with threads of blue,
Embracing the dreams that once we knew.
Whispers of shells on the soft, warm sand,
Together we wander, hand in hand.

Dancing with tides, the moon serenades,
While laughter rides on the cresting waves.
Sprinkled with stardust, desires collide,
In this ocean, we gently confide.

Coral and driftwood, treasures unearth,
Each piece a memory of oceanic birth.
Anchors of hope in the gentle tide,
Where love and freedom forever bide.

Gliding through moments, sweet currents hum,
The rhythm of life plays, softly strum.
As sunsets blaze with colors bright,
Embrace of the ocean, a lover's light.

Festooned with dreams wrapped in sea's embrace,
Every crest and trough, a heart's true place.
Lost in the dance of the evening's grace,
In the ocean's heart, we find our space.

Threaded Stories Through Aquatic Dreams

In the depths where the stories weave,
Undersea whispers, we dare believe.
Tales of wonder, in colors so bright,
Illuminate shadows, embrace the night.

Glistening pearls, secrets concealed,
Fragments of life, in dreams revealed.
With every splash, a miracle sparked,
In aquatic realms, where beauty is marked.

The tide carries echoes, soft and low,
From hearts uncharted, where passions flow.
As currents collide, our spirits soar,
Threading the stories of ocean's lore.

In twilight's glow, the horizon bends,
Whims of the sea, where time suspends.
Through every ripple, our souls entwined,
In aquatic dreams, forever defined.

So let us dive into the profound,
Discover the depths where love is found.
In woven tales, our hopes reside,
Threaded stories in the ocean's tide.

The Underwater Bounty of the Song

In depths where silence softly reigns,
The echoes of the ocean's strains.
Colorful coral dances in light,
While fishes weave their tales of flight.

The kelp sways gently, a soothing balm,
Cradling secrets, hidden and calm.
Treasure lies beneath the waves,
In a kingdom of wonders, lost braves.

Shells glisten like stars on the sand,
Each one a story, uniquely planned.
The current whispers, sweet and low,
Of journeys past that we long to know.

Anemones pulse in vibrant hues,
Amidst the blues, in endless views.
Bounty abounds in every crest,
The ocean's song, a lover's quest.

So dive with me where the mysteries dwell,
In the underwater bounty, all is well.
The symphony plays in waves so strong,
Forever we dance to the ocean's song.

Bubbles of Whimsy in the Seafloor

Bubbles rise to meet the sun's kiss,
In a world where dreams weave bliss.
Peering through the lens of the blue,
Magic awakens, ancient and true.

Tiny creatures in playful glide,
Join the dance of the ocean's tide.
A pinwheel of colors, a spiraled embrace,
Each bubble a moment in endless space.

Seashells retreat like shy little friends,
While sea stars linger, their light never ends.
Floating on currents, wild and free,
In the seafloor's wonder, we find glee.

With every pop, a tale takes flight,
Of sunken ships and lost delight.
Bubbles of whimsy, laughter does spark,
In the theater of tides, we leave our mark.

So, let us blow dreams into the deep,
Where secrets of the sea safely sleep.
In the dance of bubbles, our spirits roam,
Finding forever in this watery home.

Cradled in Currents, Lost to Time

Cradled in currents, the memories flow,
Silent serenades from long ago.
Treasures of heartbeats from ages past,
In the embrace of the sea, we're cast.

Drifting with echoes of laughter and tears,
Stories entwined through the weaving years.
Lost sailors' visions in waves that swirl,
In the vast marine realm, their dreams twirl.

Ghostly ships in the twilight gleam,
Haunted by whispers of a tranquil dream.
Threads of time in the ocean's weave,
In the depths of the blue, we believe.

An age-old dance where shadows entwine,
Cradled in currents, lost to time.
Each tide carries tales on its breath,
Of life, of love, and the dance of death.

So, join the depths where the echoes play,
In the harmony of night, in the light of day.
Forever we wander, forever we climb,
Cradled in currents, lost to time.

Driftwood and Distant Stars

Driftwood floats on azure seas,
Whispers of journeys lost in breeze.
Underneath the velvet night,
Distant stars in tranquil light.

Carved by waves, each story told,
Silhouettes in twilight bold.
A tapestry of dreams entwined,
With echoes of the heart defined.

Silent secrets in the sand,
Tracing footprints, hand in hand.
Nature's canvas, wide and free,
Guided by our shared decree.

In the moment, time stands still,
With every echo, every thrill.
The sea may change, the stars may fade,
But memories in hearts are laid.

So let the driftwood find its way,
Through the night, into the day.
With every wave, a promise near,
In distant stars, our path is clear.

Chasing Shadows of Aquatic Delights

Beneath the waves, shadows dance,
Corals sway in a vibrant trance.
Sunlight filters through the deep,
In these waters, secrets keep.

Fish flit by in colorful hues,
Each one a tale, each one a muse.
Rippling currents, whispers so sweet,
Echoes of laughter in the heat.

Shells and stones upon the shore,
Nature's beauty, to explore.
In the tide, we find our place,
Lost in dreams of ocean's grace.

Chasing ripples, hearts in flight,
Sailing through the soft, blue night.
Every splash a fleeting song,
In the depths, where we belong.

So let us wander, hand in hand,
Through this bright, enchanted land.
With the waves, we'll drift and glide,
Chasing shadows side by side.

Navigating the Currents of Time

Time flows like a gentle stream,
Moments drift, a fleeting dream.
Navigating paths unknown,
In this journey, seeds are sown.

Waves of memories crash and break,
Guiding choices we all make.
Ripples echo through the years,
Laughter mingles with our tears.

In the quiet, we find our way,
Charting courses day by day.
With every ebb, a lesson learned,
In the fire, our spirits burned.

Through the storms and calm alike,
In every twist, a guiding spike.
Time may shift, but we stand tall,
Embracing life as tides enthrall.

So let us sail on wild seas,
With open hearts, we sail with ease.
In the currents, we find our rhyme,
Forever young, through the sands of time.

A Dance of Shells and Stars

On the shore where moonlight gleams,
Shells are scattered, spun from dreams.
Whispers of the ocean's grace,
In every shell, a touch of space.

Stars above, a twinkling light,
Dancing softly through the night.
With every crest, a story spun,
Of love, of loss, of worlds begun.

The tide will shift, the waves will rise,
Reflecting stars in endless skies.
In the dance of time and fate,
We find our place, we celebrate.

As the night wraps us in peace,
Shells and stars, our hearts increase.
We'll waltz upon this sandy floor,
Forever yearning, evermore.

So let the music of the sea,
Guide us through eternity.
In the embrace of shells and stars,
We are together, near or far.

Ocean's Heirlooms and Mystical Charms

In the depths where shadows play,
Secrets of the sea dwell and sway.
Pearls glisten in twilight's embrace,
Guardians of time, hidden space.

Mystical shells carry a song,
Tales of love where hearts belong.
Dances of dolphins, soft and bright,
Guiding lost souls through the night.

Waves whisper softly, old and wise,
Under the vast, eternal skies.
Ocean's treasures, both fierce and calm,
Nature's embrace, a healing balm.

The horizon glows with golden hue,
A tapestry of dreams anew.
Each crest and trough, a story spun,
In the ocean's heart, we are one.

Past Lives in the Ocean's Embrace

Echoes of whispers in the tide,
Carried on waves, the memories ride.
Faded footprints on the sandy shore,
Revealing the lives that came before.

Ghostly ships in the moonlight wane,
Carved into wood, their silent pain.
Rustling tales of lovers lost,
In the sea's depths, there's always a cost.

The salt-kissed air remembers the past,
An endless journey that holds steadfast.
Ocean's embrace, a comforting shroud,
Encircling secrets, both soft and proud.

From seashells' echo to the deep sea's light,
The past weaves into the calming night.
Oceans cradle the dreams we've spun,
In their embrace, we become one.

Currents of Lavish Memories

As tides flow gently, memories wake,
A journey of laughter, love, and ache.
Currents of joy in a shimmering stream,
Where every wave holds a cherished dream.

Drifting on sails of nostalgia's breeze,
With skies painted gold and evening's tease.
Each ripple tells stories of days gone by,
In the ocean of thought, I learn to fly.

The wind carries whispers of ages past,
In the dance of the water, we hold fast.
Seashells clink like treasures divine,
Echoing memories, eternally entwined.

From the ocean's depth to the shore so wide,
Every current ignites the heart's tide.
Waves, like laughter, crash and swell,
In the bounty of time, I dwell.

The Allure of Oceanic Whispers

Beneath the moon's gaze, the ocean sighs,
Soft whispers swirl, like secret ties.
An enchanting lull, soothing and cool,
Guiding wild hearts like stars in a pool.

The ebb and flow of the midnight tide,
Around the rock where dreams reside.
Fingers of foam brush against the sand,
In the sea's hush, we take a stand.

Mysteries linger like mist on the shore,
Each whisper beckons, a distant lore.
Crickets sing with the waves' gentle hum,
Together we listen, to where we come from.

With each breaking wave, the past unites,
In the allure of oceanic nights.
Softly we cradle the dreams once steeped,
In the heart of the waters, promises keep.

Currents of Ancient Tales

Whispers ride the wave's embrace,
Echoes of a time long lost.
Fables woven in the foam,
Tales of ships and tempest tossed.

Glimmers of forgotten lore,
Sailors' dreams and mermaid songs.
Fragments linger on the shore,
In the surf where memory throngs.

Ancient maps and sundried sails,
Carved in stone, on ocean's floor.
Currents shift with gentle tales,
Guiding hearts to distant shores.

Beneath the moon's soft silver glow,
Secrets held in depths unknown.
Each wave carries tales to sow,
In the hearts of those who've grown.

Legends rise with every tide,
A dancer lost in sea's embrace.
Currents pull, and we abide,
Chasing dreams through time and space.

Chasing Fables in the Splashing Blue

In the morning's softest light,
Waves would play, as whispers tease.
Chasing fables, hearts take flight,
Dancing dreams upon the breeze.

Splashing blue, a painter's brush,
Coloring life with tales untold.
Each ripple sings in vibrant hush,
Brushing secrets, brave and bold.

Beneath the surf, new worlds await,
Creatures weave their ancient dance.
Chasing echoes, we tempt fate,
A symphony of wild chance.

In the twilight, shadows blend,
Sailing stories on the tide.
Wanderers, where the sea transcends,
In its depths, we confide.

Fables rise with every crest,
In the splash, our laughter blends.
Chasing dreams, we feel so blessed,
As the ocean's magic never ends.

The Siren's Castaway Delight

Under stars, where shadows play,
The siren sings a haunting tune.
Her voice weaves night into day,
As the ocean cradles the moon.

Castaways on a dreamer's quest,
Wishing on the tides' soft hum.
In her arms, we find our rest,
As waves drum softly, hearts succumb.

Glimpses of a distant shore,
Golden sands and skies so wide.
Where the sirens once did soar,
And every dreamer basks in pride.

Echoes swirl in frothy bliss,
Luring sailors, lost from sight.
In each melody, a kiss,
Guiding ships through endless night.

The siren's song, sweet as delight,
Calls to those who dare to roam.
In her embrace, the stars ignite,
For weary hearts, she is home.

Serene Tokens of Oceanic Reverie

Glistening shells on the sandy beach,
Whispers of the past invite.
Serene tokens, out of reach,
Memories dance in morning light.

Waves caress each longing heart,
With secrets swaying in their flow.
From each tide, a brand new start,
In ocean's arms, our spirits grow.

Drifting dreams in salty air,
Stars align to guide our way.
In this realm, without a care,
Oceanic reveries sway.

Mystical journeys come alive,
With every wave, a brand new tale.
In this moment, we survive,
Our hearts embrace the freedom sail.

Grains of sand, like wishes cast,
In the ocean's timeless grasp.
Serene tokens that will last,
In the waves, our dreams will clasp.

Treasures Cradled by the Waves

Upon the shore, where soft sands lie,
Glints of gold in tide pools sigh.
Seashells whisper tales of old,
Mysteries wrapped in emerald fold.

Waves caress, a gentle song,
Cradling treasures all night long.
Silver fish dart, in playful grace,
Eager hearts find their embrace.

The ocean's depth, a jeweled prize,
Hidden dreams in liquid skies.
With every rise, the secrets blend,
Nature's bounty knows no end.

In twilight's hush, the colors dance,
Reflecting beauty, an ocean's trance.
Softly beckoning, a siren's call,
To those who wander and dream, enthralled.

So gather close, the treasures near,
In waves' embrace, cast out your fear.
For the ocean's heart shall always yield,
The secrets cherished, forever sealed.

Luminous Charms of the Deep

Deep below, where shadows play,
Luminous charms light the way.
Glowing corals in hues divine,
Dance in harmony, so entwined.

Flickering lights, a starry sight,
In waters dark, they bring delight.
Gentle whispers from creatures rare,
Guide the lost with tender care.

Echoes of laughter, bubbles rise,
In this realm, the magic lies.
Softly shimmering, like dreams unfurled,
Luminous treasures of the world.

With every pulse, the sea does sing,
Of wonders vast, and the joy they bring.
Each gentle wave, a story shared,
In the depths, hearts are bared.

So dive below, embrace the glow,
Let the charms of the deep bestow.
Guiding hands of ocean's grace,
In luminous charms, find your place.

The Siren's Jewel Box

Nestled deep in the ocean's fold,
The siren sings, her secrets told.
Pearls of wisdom, treasures rare,
Hidden gems beyond compare.

Whispers echo in the salty breeze,
Drawing sailors with gentle ease.
Heartbeats quicken, as waves arise,
Captivated by those haunting cries.

In glimmering depths, where shadows sway,
The jewel box of the sea does lay.
Each glint a promise, a wish bestowed,
In fragrant swirls of sea foam flowed.

Seashell trinkets, stories they share,
Of distant lands and hearts laid bare.
Unlock the box, let wonder flow,
And you may find what you yearn to know.

With every tide, the treasures change,
Yet the siren's song will not estrange.
In this jewel box, dreams take flight,
Guided by the moon's soft light.

Echoes of Sunlit Shores

Footprints trace the golden sands,
Echoes play in gentle hands.
Waves recede, a soft caress,
Laughter dances in summer's dress.

Seagulls cry in breezy flight,
Chasing shadows, hearts alight.
Shells like whispers, buried deep,
Guarding stories they will keep.

Sunset paints the sky ablaze,
Golden hues in evening's gaze.
Twilight wraps the world in peace,
Where the echoes never cease.

With each tide, new tales unfurl,
Of love and loss in the ocean's swirl.
Let the sunlit shores imbue,
A melody sweet, eternally true.

So linger here, where echoes play,
Bathe in the golden end of day.
For sunlit shores shall always sing,
The timeless joy that memories bring.

Whispers of Pearl and Ocean Blue

Whispers dance on gentle tides,
Secrets held where beauty hides.
The ocean's voice, a soft embrace,
In azure depths, a sacred place.

Pearl treasures glimmer in the light,
Mysteries veiled from mortal sight.
Each wave a song that beckons near,
The whispers call to those who hear.

The sun dips low, a fiery hue,
Brushing waves in shades anew.
With every tide, a tale unfolds,
In ocean's heart, the truth it holds.

Beneath the surface, shadows play,
Nature's art in grand ballet.
As currents weave through time and space,
The whispers blend with ocean's grace.

In tranquil dreams, the waters flow,
Carrying secrets we long to know.
With every breath, we drift and sway,
In whispers of pearl, we find our way.

Lure of the Sunken Secrets

Underneath the rolling waves,
Lie the stories, silent graves.
A siren's call, alluring, sweet,
The sunken secrets, whispers fleet.

Ancient ships in coral beds,
Echoes of forgotten threads.
A treasure map in shadows drawn,
Each wreckage hides a whispered dawn.

Glimmers shine through azure blue,
A dance of light, a beckoning view.
Beneath the depths, the silence hums,
The lure of mysteries yet to come.

Adventurers with hearts so bold,
Chase the tales that time has told.
In watery realms, our dreams take flight,
Unraveling secrets in the night.

The depths a canvas, grand and wide,
With every dive, our fears subside.
Each secret found, a treasure's gain,
In sunken depths, we break the chain.

The Allure of the Azure Depths

In the embrace of azure waves,
The ocean sings, the spirit braves.
Tales of wonder, depths unknown,
In every ripple, life is sown.

Creatures dance in liquid light,
Shadows shifting, pure delight.
Beneath the surface, magic swirls,
A hidden world of ocean pearls.

Colors blend in twilight's kiss,
A symphony of tranquil bliss.
The azure depths call out to me,
To dive and drift, to roam so free.

The stars above, the stars below,
In the deep, our souls will flow.
With every heartbeat, we explore,
The allure pulls us more and more.

In azure dreams, we intertwine,
Our spirits dance, our hearts align.
In ocean's embrace, we find our peace,
The allure of depths will never cease.

Captivated by the Dance of Waves

Captivated by the dance of waves,
Nature's rhythm, wild and brave.
Each crest and trough, a timeless art,
The ocean's beat, a living heart.

With every surge, our worries fade,
In the water's flow, our fears betrayed.
The salty kiss, the cool caress,
In waves we find our true finesse.

A ballet bold, a fluid grace,
The dance of water, nature's embrace.
With whispered secrets in the foam,
The ocean's spirit calls us home.

To ride the swell, to soar and glide,
In harmony, we turn the tide.
The dance ignites a primal spark,
Together we carve our mark.

As twilight casts its golden hue,
The ocean whispers, calm and true.
In every wave, a heartbeat flows,
Captured in time, the dance bestows.

Luminous Secrets in Coral Caves

In the depths, colors dance bright,
Whispers of magic in soft twilight.
Hidden worlds where shadows play,
Coral secrets, night and day.

Gentle currents weave through walls,
Luminous wonders, nature's calls.
Fishes glimmer like stars afar,
Guiding dreamers to where they are.

Echoes of silence, a tranquil song,
Where the lost and found belong.
Beneath the waves, stories unfold,
In coral caves, treasures untold.

A tapestry woven in ocean's embrace,
Timeless tales of a sacred place.
Emerald greens and ruby reds,
The vibrant heart where life spreads.

Seek the treasures, delve within,
In these caves, the journey begins.
Luminous secrets, a gift to behold,
In the depths of the deep, let tales be told.

Shimmering Dreams in Saltwater

Waves in rhythm, a soothing sound,
Shimmering dreams where hope is found.
Saltwater kisses, the breeze's sigh,
Under the vast, open sky.

Footprints marked on the shifting sand,
Stories of love, each grain a strand.
Seashell secrets that whisper sweet,
With every tide, new dreams greet.

Glistening horizons, horizons so wide,
In the depths of blue, emotions abide.
Dreamers wander with hearts so light,
Dancing through shadows, chasing the light.

Sunset hues blend, a vibrant spread,
Painting the sky where wishes are fed.
Nature's canvas displays its art,
Saltwater dreams, a longing heart.

Calming ripples, a lullaby's trace,
In saltwater realms, we find our place.
Holding the magic that waves will weave,
In shimmering dreams, we dare to believe.

Stories Told by Ocean's Bounty

Whispers of tides, what tales they share,
Ocean's bounty, secrets laid bare.
From shell to wave, each speaks of time,
Nature's language, a rhythmic rhyme.

Harvested moments found in the deep,
A treasure of stories, both yours and mine.
Fish shimmering like stars in the night,
Guiding our hearts to the ocean's light.

Sunrise tales over aqua blue,
Where legends linger, ancient and new.
Each surf's caress tells of the past,
In the bounty of waves, memories last.

Gathered shells, with narratives bold,
Echoing wisdom that never grows old.
From stormy squalls to serene tides,
Ocean's bounty, where truth resides.

Chasing horizons, forever we seek,
Stories of solace in the sea's mystique.
An endless saga, rich and profound,
In the ocean's arms, a treasure is found.

Hidden Gems on Wavelit Shores

Footprints hidden, lost in time,
Wavelit shores, where dreams align.
Golden grains beneath our feet,
A treasure trove, so bittersweet.

Shells, soft whispers from the sea,
Telling secrets of what might be.
Beneath the tide, magic resides,
In the gems that the ocean hides.

Sunrise glimmers on the foam,
Wavelit paths, where wanderers roam.
With every wave, a promise made,
In time's embrace, our fears allayed.

Stepping lightly on this shore,
Finding treasures, wanting more.
Seaweed jewels, wild and free,
Each hidden gem, a mystery.

Sands of time, like fleeting dreams,
Hold the magic within their seams.
Among the waves, we find our place,
In hidden gems, a warm embrace.

A Symphony of Sea and Silver

The waves dance softly on the shore,
While moonlight weaves a silken score.
Stars shimmer in a velvet sky,
Whispers of the ocean sigh.

Shells sparkle like jewels in the sand,
Crafted with care by nature's hand.
Seashells echo stories untold,
Of mermaid dreams and treasures bold.

The breeze carries tunes of delight,
Where the sea meets the stars at night.
A symphony, pure and divine,
With each wave, a heartbeat entwined.

Secrets lie in the depths so blue,
In shadows where the sun's light withdrew.
Seafoam kisses the shore with grace,
Embracing the night in an endless embrace.

The Mariner's Tryst with Lost Relics

In twilight's glow, the ships do rest,
The mariner dreams of a sunken quest.
Old maps whisper of treasures deep,
Where the ocean's secrets quietly sleep.

A compass spins, drawn by the tide,
Guiding the way where old ghosts glide.
Amber and gold in coral's hold,
Tales of adventure waiting to unfold.

With each dive, the past comes alive,
Ghostly ships where memories thrive.
Relics glimmer, artful and grand,
Carried ashore by the dreaming sand.

Moonlit paths guide the weary soul,
In search of a heart that's long lost whole.
Echoes of laughter on ocean's crest,
A tryst with history—the mariner's rest.

Seaside Visions in Ethereal Glow

In the dawn's embrace, the waves alight,
Caressing the shore in soft morning light.
Seagulls cry as they dance in flight,
A canvas of dreams by the ocean's height.

Ethereal hues paint the sky,
Pink and gold, as day draws nigh.
Gentle whispers of salt in the air,
Seaside visions, beyond compare.

Footprints trace where hearts have roamed,
Each grain of sand, a story of home.
Driftwood memories on the tide,
Nature's artistry, a true guide.

The horizon glimmers with hope anew,
Waves carry wishes, a timeless view.
In this tranquil moment, we find our place,
Seaside visions, a warm embrace.

Veiled Treasures of the Undersea World

Beneath the waves, a kingdom sleeps,
Veiled treasures in the ocean's keeps.
Coral castles and gardens thrive,
Where echoes of ancient tales come alive.

Glistening pearls wrapped in seaweed's hold,
Mysteries shimmer, worth their weight in gold.
Creatures of wonder in colors bright,
Dance in the shadows, a magical sight.

The ocean's breath sings a lullaby,
Weaving stories as tides rise high.
Lost ships beckon with whispered lore,
Veiled treasures waiting to be explored.

In currents swift, secrets flow,
Wonders hidden, the depths bestow.
An undersea realm, enigmatic and grand,
Where dreams and realities intertwine on the sand.

Soft Call of the Aquatic Gems

Beneath the waves, whispers sing,
Colors swirl in a watery ring.
Treasures lie in silence deep,
Where secrets of the ocean keep.

Corals bloom in soft embrace,
Fishes dart in a graceful race.
Echoes call from the ocean's heart,
A tranquil realm, a work of art.

Luminous orbs under starlit skies,
Dancing gently, with tranquil sighs.
Nature's jewels, gems of the sea,
Wrapped in stories, wild and free.

Waves brush softly, a gentle caress,
In this world, we find our rest.
A symphony of tides that blend,
Each moment, the ocean's friend.

Dive into wonders, let spirits soar,
In the depths, we discover more.
With each tide, a soft call remains,
A dance of dreams where peace reigns.

Ephemeral Beauty in Tidal Waves

Seashells glisten on the shore,
Tides recede and then restore.
Nature's fleeting, perfect art,
Whispers of a sailor's heart.

Sunset hues embrace the night,
A canvas washed in colors bright.
The ebb and flow, a timeless dance,
Moments gifted, not left to chance.

In each ripple, stories dwell,
Of ancient seas, they weave and swell.
Catch the beauty, let it glow,
In the heart of waves, love can grow.

Like whispers carried by the breeze,
Ephemeral, as time can freeze.
In the tide's embrace, we find,
A fleeting glimpse that lingers behind.

Hold the beauty, do not stray,
In shimmering tides, night meets day.
Every wave a dance, a tune,
Ephemeral beauty beneath the moon.

Glimmering Hopes in Fisherman's Nets

At dawn's first light, nets cast wide,
Fishermen gather with hopes and pride.
Each tangling line, a wish they weave,
In ocean's bounty, they believe.

Glimmering scales, treasures inside,
Anticipation in the rising tide.
With every catch, stories unfurl,
In the salty winds, dreams swirl.

Waves crash hard against the boat,
Songs of the sea, the fishermen wrote.
In laughter shared, the crew stands tall,
With unity, they conquer all.

The ocean gives, the ocean takes,
In its embrace, the heart awakes.
Beneath the sun, hopes align,
In nets that glimmer, futures shine.

With gentle hands, they mend and sew,
In every net, a love will grow.
Casting dreams beneath the skies,
Glimmering hopes, where courage flies.

Mementos from Depths Uncharted

From shadows deep, old tales arise,
Whispers carried on ocean's sighs.
Mementos lost beneath the foam,
In the depths, they find a home.

Ancient shipwrecks, stories told,
Carved in sand, covered in gold.
Fragments linger, hearts remember,
Each treasure holds the light of ember.

Coral gardens, wild and free,
Guardians of the deep blue sea.
Cradle memories in their arms,
Safety found in nature's charms.

Mysterious depths lure us close,
In shadows where the light can boast.
With each dive, we seek to learn,
The tales of tides and twists that turn.

Beneath the waves lies history's thread,
In silent depths, we trace the dead.
Mementos float where secrets dwell,
In ocean's heart, we hear their bell.

Pearls of Ancient Epics

In shadows deep, the heroes rose,
With whispered tales, the ancient prose.
They battled fate, with swords in hand,
And etched their names upon the sand.

Legends carved in the stars above,
Woven with courage, honor, and love.
In every heart a secret burns,
A treasure found, a lesson learned.

The moonlight danced on pages worn,
Of dreams fulfilled and hopes reborn.
Each verse a gem, a timeless sign,
Of stories shared through space and time.

From whispers soft, the echoes grow,
Of battles fought and rivers flowed.
In ancient winds, their voices weave,
A tapestry where we believe.

So let us gather 'round the fire,
And share these tales, our hearts inspire.
For in each word, a world appears,
In pearls of wisdom through the years.

Charmed by the Currents of Story

In rivers wide, the tales drift slow,
With currents strong, they ebb and flow.
Each story's thread a winding stream,
Where dreams cascade and spirits gleam.

A whisper grows, the waters dance,
Timeless rhythms in a spellbound trance.
From local lore to distant lands,
In every heart, a legend stands.

The beckoning waves sing of yore,
Of heroes brave and ancient lore.
With every twist, a lesson flows,
In currents deep, our courage grows.

From ashes rise the dreams anew,
United paths of me and you.
In every word, the currents guide,
A journey vast, a flowing tide.

So take my hand and wander far,
On history's streams, beneath the stars.
Charmed by tales, we sail and soar,
In rivers deep, forevermore.

Medleys of Light and Shadow Beneath

Beneath the surface, secrets hide,
In shadows cast, where dreams collide.
A dance of light and darkness play,
As stories blend and drift away.

The echoes stir in silent depths,
Where whispers dwell and time reflects.
With every flicker, a tale unfolds,
In twilight's grasp, the truth beholds.

Medleys weave in the stillness found,
With gentle sighs, the heartbeats sound.
In hidden worlds, both bold and bright,
The shadows speak of total light.

Through layers thick, we journey on,
Collecting fragments till they're gone.
For what's unseen is also real,
In every shade, we learn to feel.

So let us plumb these depths so wide,
Discover worlds that bide inside.
With every step, a spark ignites,
Medleys of truth, our spirits' flights.

The Rhythm of Forgotten Sapphire Shores

On sapphire shores where whispers call,
The rhythm beats through rise and fall.
With every wave, a story sings,
Of ancient tides and timeless things.

The sands hold dreams of those who tread,
With every step, the past is fed.
Footprints linger, then fade away,
In ocean's breath, night turns to day.

Unseen, the dance beneath the blue,
A harmony that feels quite true.
The shells and stones all share their lore,
In echoes soft along the shore.

So let the sea guide you to find,
The endless rhythm of the mind.
For in its depths, all tales abide,
On sapphire shores, where dreams reside.

From sun-kissed dawn to twilight's grace,
The rhythm flows in this embrace.
With every tide, let go, explore,
The forgotten songs forevermore.

Whims of the Ocean's Heart

In the deep blue's sway, dreams arise,
Waves whisper secrets, soft lullabies.
Dancing with shadows, the tides take flight,
Unraveling wonders, in day and night.

Colors of coral, vibrant and bright,
Fish weave through currents, pure delight.
Echoes of laughter, carried afar,
Sculpting the shores like a wandering star.

Gulls cry above, in joyous refrain,
While seashells gather the gentle rain.
On the horizon, sunsets ignite,
The ocean's heart beats, wild and light.

Castles in sand, built strong and high,
Waves kiss the edges, they sigh goodbye.
Moments are fleeting, yet vivid they seem,
Caught in the vastness, like a cherished dream.

Every swell tells a tale, unique,
In every ripple, ancient voices speak.
The whims of the ocean, forever untold,
In whispers of water, their mysteries unfold.

Glimmers in the Moonlit Waters

Silver reflections dance on the sea,
Whispers of magic, a soft decree.
Stars spark a fire, in twilight's embrace,
Moonlit adventure, a secret place.

Tides pull and push, in rhythmic grace,
Dreams float on waves, in a mystical chase.
Crickets sing softly, a serenade,
As shadows of night serenely invade.

Ripples of light, like diamonds afloat,
In the hush of the night, their stories wrote.
Magic unfolds, with each gentle crest,
Carried by currents, the ocean's quest.

Soft lull of the waters, a soothing hymn,
While starlight glistens, beginnings brim.
In moon's embrace, the world feels new,
Glimmers of wonder, in midnight's hue.

Here under the cosmos, hearts intertwine,
Lost in the moment, enchanted by signs.
Where dreams collide, and reality bends,
In moonlit waters, the adventure never ends.

Tales in the Shell's Melodic Chime

Curled in the sand, a treasure resides,
Whispers of ocean in each shell abides.
A song from the depths, a story untold,
In the cradle of nature, its secrets behold.

Listen closely, to the echoes of time,
Each swirl and each curve holds rhythm and rhyme.
The tides weave a tapestry, vast and wide,
In the shell's embrace, past memories hide.

Voices of waves sing of journeys long,
In the chorus of shells, nature's sweet song.
Each chime a reminder of places once seen,
In the heart of the ocean, where dreams come to glean.

Tiny adventures in spirals confined,
Hope tied to journeys, forever aligned.
Through the soft murmurs, we hear their charm,
The tales of the sea, both soothing and warm.

Gather these whispers, let them bestow,
Wisdom of waters that ebb and flow.
In each little shell, a world to explore,
Tales of the ocean, forever encore.

Hidden Prizes Cradled in Foam

Foamy caresses kiss the warm shore,
Hiding the treasures, washed up and more.
Glistening gems spark the wanderer's gaze,
In nature's bounty, the heart warms and sways.

Smooth stones and fragments of ships long gone,
Stories of sailors, their hopes drawn upon.
Scattered below the soft sand's embrace,
Hidden prizes found, in time and space.

Seaglass like sunlight, twinkling so bright,
Reflecting the dreams of the ocean's light.
Each piece a memory, a moment to hold,
Whispers of journeys, both daring and bold.

Along the coastline, where land meets the sea,
Every wave brings forth what's meant to be.
In the laughter of gulls, in the kids' delight,
Hidden prizes shine under the sky so bright.

In the ebb and flow, life's secrets abide,
Cradled in foam, where the wonders collide.
Every visit a treasure, every footprint a song,
In nature's playground, together we belong.

www.ingramcontent.com/pod-product-compliance
Ingram Content Group UK Ltd.
Pitfield, Milton Keynes, MK11 3LW, UK
UKHW021632200125
4187UKWH00003B/100

9 781805 593683